HR STAMPED
WAYS TO TELL
COWORKERS
THEY'RE STUPID
(OFFICIALLY APPROVED)

Welcome to the Corporate Circus

Congratulations! You've survived another day
in the workplace and found this book. Whether
you're here to laugh at your coworkers, vent your
frustrations, or secretly confirm that you're not
the problem (spoiler: you might be), you're in the
right place.

This book is a celebration of office quirks, workplace chaos, and the universal truths we all en-
dure in the 9-to-5 grind. If you recognize yourself
in these pages... well, maybe it's time to schedule
a meeting with yourself.

Now, grab a coffee (but don't steal someone
else's), find a quiet corner (good luck with that),
and enjoy the ride.

Note to HR (if you're reading this): Don't worry,
this book is completely harmless. Just like that
sticky note on the breakroom fridge.

The Coffee Rationer

Three drops left? Wow, What a gift. Truly, you're a saint.

HR CLEARED

When the pot is this low, it's usually best to start a fresh brew for the team.

Perfect for when the coworker leaves exactly 0.3 nanoliters of coffee in the pot, kept warm for two hours until it develops the consistency of tar. Watch them defend this act with "I thought someone might want the rest" while avoiding eye contact with the line of caffeine-deprived coworkers forming behind them.

The Break Room DJ

Oh, you thought the office needed a soundtrack? How thoughtful.

HR CLEARED

The break room is a shared space – I didn't realize 'shared workspace' translated to 'personal concert venue.'

Perfect for the coworker who turns their phone speaker into the office boombox, playing TikToks, Instagram Reels, and that one remix of Baby Shark at full volume. They laugh at their videos so hard you wonder if they're trying to summon the dead. Bonus points if they pause the video to explain the joke to you, as if you're dying to know why yet another cat video changed their life.

The Lunch Raider

This is the coworker who treats the fridge like their own personal buffet. They specialize in stealing the most exciting item in the fridge (always yours), then pretending they thought it was communal property. "Oh, I didn't realize this was yours—sorry!" Their performance art peaks when confronted. They'll gasp in shock, as if the sandwich magically appeared in their hand.

The Break Room CEO

YOUR INNER VOICE

Oh, you thought the break room was your corner office? Bold move.

HR CLEARED

There are designated meeting spaces available for calls and discussions—let's use the break room for relaxation and meals!

This is the coworker who transforms the break room into their personal HQ, complete with an open laptop blaring a Zoom call on speakerphone. They shush anyone microwaving their lunch because it's "disrupting the flow," while simultaneously using the microwave timer as their project deadline tracker.

The Guardian of Mystery Tupperware

HR CLEARED

Let's regularly check and remove old items from the fridge to keep it clean and organized for everyone!

This is for the coworker who forgets their food in the fridge until it becomes a science project. Their Tupperware is full of unidentifiable sludge, and their yogurt expiration date predates the office copier. They'll argue, "Oh, I was going to eat that!" as you're scraping mold off the shelf. Pro tip: Start leaving sticky notes that say, "Your food called—it's planning its escape."

[Name] is typing...

Just admit you haven't done it and stop wasting my damn time with those dancing dots.

HR CLEARED

I'm patiently awaiting your carefully crafted response.

This is your moment when someone has been typing, deleting, and retyping for so long that you've mentally drafted your retirement speech. For extra fun, message them "Everything okay?" right before they finally hit send and watch as they start over.

The Reptile Detective

YOUR INNER VOICE

You absolute trainwreck. You can't even take a fcking screenshot without exposing that you're googling 'Is my boss secretly a lizard person'.

HR CLEARED

I received your screenshot. Would you like to resend a more focused version?

Perfect for when a coworker sends you a screenshot, unaware their tabs are broadcasting their panic over your boss's suspiciously reptilian behaviors—like maintaining uncomfortably long eye contact, cranking the office thermostat to "basking temperature," or that tongue-flicking thing during presentations. Let them marinate in the horror. If they try to explain, just reply: "No worries, we all have... curiosities."

The Emergency Evaporator

'Emergency!' And then... silence. Classic you.

HR CLEARED

I saw your urgent message from two hours ago. I trust since I haven't heard back, the situation has been resolved?

Perfect for when the coworker detonates a verbal flare with "HELP!!" at 10:23 AM, evaporates into the ether, and reemerges at 1:47 PM with a casual "nvm fixed it :)." Meanwhile, you've been refreshing Slack so hard your mouse filed a workers' comp claim. Classic coworker—chaos in the streets, zen in the replies.

The Text Avalanche

Did your Enter key die in a tragic accident, or do you enjoy torturing people with this unformatted mess? This looks like a ransom note written by an energetic squirrel on espresso.

HR CLEARED

Thanks for the detailed message. Would you mind breaking this down into key points for better tracking?

Perfect for when the coworker unleashes a 500-word stream of consciousness in chat—no paragraphs, no punctuation, just pure chaos. Reading it feels like deciphering a legal document written during a midlife crisis. If the coworker refuses to format, respond with your own unbroken wall of text about the importance of clear communication.

The Instruction Ignorer

The guide is literally pinned, but sure, let me drop everything so I can spoon-feed you basic instructions.

HR CLEARED

Sure thing! Here's the documentation that explains it step-by-step. I'll wait here in case it mysteriously vanishes while you're reading.

Perfect for when a coworker skips the blindingly obvious pinned document (or the one emailed, book-marked, and tattooed on the team wiki) and still asks you to explain it like you're their personal audiobook. Extra fun when they say, "Ohhh, I didn't realize this was here," as if the pinned icon is somehow written in invisible ink.

The Paper Phantom

Cool, I'll just conjure paper out of thin air while you vanish like Houdini.

HR CLEARED

Let's refill the printer tray when it's empty to keep things running smoothly for everyone!

This is the coworker who burns through an entire ream of paper, then leaves the tray empty like it's someone else's problem. They'll disappear just as you're trying to print something important, leaving you to frantically hunt for paper while silently cursing their existence. Bonus points if they leave one sad, crumpled sheet in the tray to avoid being officially responsible.

The Courtesy Looper

HR CLEARED

Perhaps we could establish a speaking order, unless we'd prefer to turn this into an extended exercise in corporate courtesy?

For when two polite coworkers get stuck in an endless "No, you go ahead" loop. The time vortex of apologies can trap everyone for minutes. Watch as they trade "Please, after you" like they're playing politeness ping-pong. The meeting grinds to a halt while they per-form this ritual of excessive courtesy. Neither wants to seem rude by actually speaking, so instead they waste everyone's time being aggressively consider-ate.

The Nostril Broadcaster

HR CLEARED

Your current camera angle certainly provides a unique perspective. Perhaps we could explore a setup that allows us to see more than just your dental work?

For the coworker who accidentally turns every meeting into a nostril exploration documentary. Their webcam always finds that perfect angle where ceiling fans and nasal passages become the stars of the show. Watch everyone politely pretend not to notice this unique perspective while they chat away. Their laptop seems to have only two positions: "extreme up-nose" or "mysterious ceiling corner." They've been in virtual meetings for years but still haven't discovered the "camera preview" option.

The Question Hydra

HR CLEARED

Your enthusiasm for clarity is remarkable! Perhaps we could schedule a follow-up session to dive deeper into your remaining 16... quick questions?

For the coworker who turns Q&A into an endless saga. They ask questions that multiply like rabbits – each answer spawns three more "quick follow-ups." Watch the presenter's hope die as they hear "Just one more thing" for the sixth time. They somehow store an infinite supply of increasingly detailed questions, yet never remember to ask them before the final two minutes of any meeting.

The Five-Minute Scholar

HR CLEARED

Your thorough research into the first Google result is impressive. Perhaps we could explore a few additional sources for a more nuanced perspective?

For the coworker who presents hastily googled facts like they're a leading expert. They confidently share information they learned approximately three minutes before the meeting. Watch them stumble when asked anything beyond the first paragraph of Wikipedia. Their "extensive research" involves skimming one article and maybe glancing at its images. They use phrases like "studies show" and "experts agree" without being able to name a single study or expert.

The Desk Decorator (Excessive)

HR CLEARED

Your personal touches really make this space unique! Maybe we could chat about keeping work areas comfy for everyone.

For the coworker whose desk looks like a yard sale exploded. Their workspace is buried under bobbleheads, family photos, and enough scented candles. Their decorations are slowly taking over neighboring desks like an invasive species. During meetings, everyone wonders if the twinkling lights or the motion-activated singing fish is worse for their growing headache.

The Pen Chewer

HR CLEARED

Perhaps we could order some stress balls for the office to help with focus during intense work periods!

For the coworker who turns pens into chew toys. They hand back borrowed pens looking like they survived a garbage disposal. During meetings, everyone watches in horror as they mindlessly gnaw plastic into abstract art. The worst part? They seem shocked when someone points it out, as if the tooth marks appeared by magic.

The Nail Clipper

HR CLEARED

Quick reminder that personal grooming
works best in the restroom!

For the coworker who thinks shared spaces are perfect for impromptu nail salon time. The sharp click-click makes everyone flinch like a horror movie jump scare. They always pick the worst moments – during lunch or important phone calls. Watch other coworkers develop ninja-like reflexes, diving for cover at the first sign of nail clippers emerging from a drawer.

The Snack Rusker

HR CLEARED

Quiet snack options help maintain a focused work environment!

For the coworker who selects snacks based on maximum decibel potential. They open bags with the stealth of a tornado, then crunch each chip like they're auditioning for a sound effects role. Watch them somehow make eating a single carrot sound like woodpeckers attacking metal. Their snacking intensity increases during conference calls and moments of deep concentration around them.

The Print-zilla

HR CLEARED

Digital copies save paper and help our green office goals!

For the coworker who treats the printer like their best friend. They print everything – emails, calendar invites, and memes they could just look at on screen. During the office "Save the Planet" meeting, they nodded along while printing the entire presentation – one slide per page, color, single-sided. The printer makes a special groaning sound when it sees them coming.

The Stationery Hoarder

YOUR INNER VOICE

Got enough sticky notes there? Planning to wallpaper your house?

HR CLEARED

Let's make sure everyone can find supplies when they need them!

For the coworker whose desk hides more office supplies than the supply room itself. They sneak to the cabinet like they're pulling a heist, walking away with handfuls of pens and paper clips. Ask them for a highlighter and watch them get weirdly protective, reluctantly handing one over while keeping an eye on it like you might run off with their prized possession.

The Office Supply Borrow-And-Never-Returner

Ah yes, the black hole where staplers go to die. Do you collect them like Pokémon?

HR CLEARED

A quick checkout system might help everyone find the tools they need!

For the coworker who thinks "borrow" means "keep forever." Their desk collects staplers, scissors, and tape dispensers like trophies. Their famous line "Just need this for a sec!" is the biggest lie in office history. Veteran coworkers now write desperate notes on their supplies or literally chain items to their desks like they're guarding the crown jewels.

The Alarm Setter (Multiple)

YOUR INNER VOICE

Is this an office or a fire drill testing facility? Pick a time and stick with it!

HR CLEARED

Silent vibration modes on phones can help maintain our peaceful work environment!

For the coworker whose phone erupts in alarms every 15 minutes. They set reminders for everything – lunch, coffee, breathing – with the volume cranked to "wake the dead." They're never at their desk when these atomic bomb sirens go off, leaving everyone else to enjoy the full symphony of beeps and pop songs that continue for eternity because they never learned how the snooze button works.

The Desk Exerciser

HR CLEARED

Our wellness room might be perfect for those energy-boosting activities!

For the coworker who treats their cubicle like a personal fitness studio. They do chair squats during conference calls and desktop push-ups while waiting for emails to load. Their aggressive stretching routine has nearly taken out three monitors and one intern. Everyone holds their coffee cups tightly when the midday yoga poses begin, knowing the downward dog might become a domino effect of disaster across neighboring workspaces.

The Overly Enthusiastic Morning Person

It's 8 AM. Nobody needs jazz hands before coffee. Nobody.

HR CLEARED

Your energy is wonderful! Maybe we could dial it to match others who are still waking up?

For the coworker who bounces in at 7 AM like they've been mainlining espresso since dawn. They're singing "Good morning!" while most people are still trying to remember their own names. They start team meetings with "Isn't it a BEAUTIFUL day?" while everyone else silently fantasizes about tripping them on their next cheerful lap around the office. Their volume knob seems permanently stuck at "outdoor concert" until at least noon.

The Excessive Pacer

HR CLEARED

The conference rooms are great for calls
that require movement or deep thinking!

For the coworker who can't sit still during calls and
creates their own racetrack around the office. Their
pacing pattern is so predictable you could set your
watch by it. Everyone has developed a sixth sense for
when they'll appear around a corner, phone pressed
to ear, gesturing wildly. The carpet has actual worn
paths that maintenance keeps trying to fix.

The Name Mispronouncer

For the coworker who treats names like they're optional tongue-twisters. They've been introduced to "Megan" at least 40 times but still say "Meagan," "Morgan," or inexplicably, "Marjorie." They'll mangle the same names in three different ways during one meeting, then look confused when corrected. Their crowning achievement is confidently introducing people incorrectly to clients, creating a chain reaction of awkward corrections that derails entire presentations.

The Desk Stalker

HR CLEARED

When you need my attention, a quick message lets me prepare for our conversation!

For the coworker who lurks behind you like a horror movie villain. They appear silently, somehow standing inches from your chair, watching your screen without announcing themselves. You'll be typing away when suddenly a voice from above asks, "Whatcha working on?" causing your soul to leave your body. They lean in so close during discussions that you can identify their lunch and toothpaste brand from their breath alone.

The Meeting Doodler

For the coworker who turns every meeting into their personal art show. Their notepad looks like a comic book exploded, complete with dragons eating the quarterly numbers. They flip pages dramatically, making everyone lose focus wondering what masterpiece is emerging. The real kicker? When asked a question, they look up startled, clearly having missed the last 20 minutes while perfecting the shading on their doodle of the boss as a superhero.

The Food Obsessed

If I hear about your keto journey one more time, I might staple my ears shut.

HR CLEARED

The break room might be the perfect spot for our more detailed food discussions!

For the coworker who turns every conversation into a food documentary. They interrupt project discussions to announce they're "doing intermittent fasting" for the fifth time that hour. Lunch breaks become TED talks about their air fryer discoveries. They circle meeting rooms like a shark when there's leftover catering, providing detailed commentary on every bite they take. Their food photos have their own separate cloud storage account due to volume.

The Pet Obsessed

HR CLEARED

Your pets sound wonderful! Maybe we could share photos during break time?

For the coworker whose entire personality is "pet parent." Their phone contains 15,000 nearly identical photos of their dog sleeping, which they'll show you unprompted. They interrupt meetings to share that their lizard did "the cutest thing" this morning. Client calls include random facts about their parrot's vocabulary. They genuinely can't understand why everyone doesn't want to hear about Fluffy's latest hairball adventure.

The "Just Joking" Offender

HR CLEARED

Our team values creating a comfortable environment where everyone feels respected!

For the coworker who uses "just kidding" like a get-out-of-jail-free card. They drop commentary that makes the room temperature drop 20 degrees, then add "lighten up!" when they see everyone's horrified faces. They've mastered the art of saying wildly inappropriate things followed by awkward laughter, as if that erases what came before. Watch them panic when someone actually calls them out, cycling through "it was a joke," "you're too sensitive," and "nobody has a sense of humor anymore" in record time.

The Keyboard Crusher

For the coworker who attacks their keyboard like it personally insulted their family. Each keystroke sounds like a small explosion, making everyone jump during quiet moments. They somehow type louder when the office is peaceful, their aggressive CLACK-CLACK-CLACK drowning out phone calls and thoughts alike. They're genuinely confused when people flinch as they start typing, completely unaware that their emails sound like they're being written with a hammer and chisel.

The Sticky Note Bomber

HR CLEARED

Direct conversations often work better than written notes for addressing concerns!

For the coworker who communicates exclusively through brightly colored sticky notes. The refrigerator looks like a ransom note collage thanks to their messages about expired yogurt. They leave cheery pink notes with thinly veiled threats about printer paper replacement. Their masterpiece? The carefully constructed pyramid of yellow stickies on your monitor reminding you about a meeting that was already on your calendar. Most notes end with a smiley face that somehow feels more menacing than friendly.

The Camera Dodger

HR CLEARED

Video participation helps create connection during our remote discussions!

For the coworker who's just a voice and a default icon during every video call. They could be lounging in pajamas, secretly at the beach, or possibly not even human. They chime in with "Sorry, my camera's not working today" for the 87th consecutive meeting. Everyone silently wonders if they're actually building a fort, or if they've been replaced by an advanced AI.

The Technical Clueless

YOUR INNER VOICE

How are you still employed in a digital workplace when you think 'the cloud' means bad weather?

HR CLEARED

Our IT team offers great one-on-one sessions that might be helpful for building tech confidence!

For the coworker who treats computers like alien technology. They've turned "Can you help me with something quick?" into a daily horror show. They click "Reply All" on company-wide emails to say "Thanks." Their desktop has 100 unnamed documents saved directly to it. Their greatest hits include accidentally muting themselves for an entire presentation, printing single emails in triplicate, and regularly asking where the "any" key is located on their keyboard.

The Microwave Mangler

What died in there? And why are you walking away from the crime scene?

HR CLEARED

A quick wipe-down after heating helps keep our shared kitchen spaces ready for everyone!

For the coworker who uses the microwave like they've never heard of lids or paper towels. They heat fish at 10 AM, creating a smell that lingers until next Tuesday. Their spaghetti sauce explosions look like evidence from a crime scene. They open the door, see the aftermath of their food bomb, then shrug and walk away. The break room now has a detailed cleaning chart with pictures because of them, yet they still manage to leave soup splatter on the ceiling.

The Bathroom Occupier

For the coworker who treats the bathroom stall like a private retreat. They disappear for stretches so long that people consider filing a missing persons report. They bring their phone, creating an unsettling soundtrack of notification pings and video sounds. The line forms outside as they settle in for what appears to be a full-length movie. They emerge looking refreshed, completely oblivious to the bathroom traffic jam they've caused.

The Thermostat Dictator

For the coworker who treats the thermostat like their personal property. They sneak over to adjust it when they think nobody's looking, leaving fingerprints as evidence. Office workers have evolved into seasonal wardrobes – sweaters and blankets in summer, tank tops in winter – because of their thermal terrorism. They complain "it's freezing in here" while everyone else is visibly sweating.

The Window Seat Defender

I didn't realize we had assigned seating based on medieval land rights.

HR CLEARED

Our flexible workspace encourages trying different areas to foster creativity!

For the coworker who has mentally engraved their name on a particular spot. They arrive obscenely early to claim "their" chair, leaving territorial markers like sweaters and coffee mugs. If someone innocently sits in their sacred space, they hover awkwardly until the intruder feels the burning stare. They've perfected passive-aggressive comments like "Oh, you're sitting here today?" with a tone that suggests you've stolen their inheritance rather than a chair by the window.

The Desk Food Stasher

HR CLEARED

Sealed containers help keep our workspace fresh and pest-free!

For the coworker who maintains a survival bunker of food in their desk. Their drawer rattles with ancient granola bars and mysterious unmarked containers. They've got enough snacks to survive an apocalypse, yet still raid the breakroom when free food appears. The mysterious smell emanating from their workspace has become stronger than their perfume. Maintenance has traced the office ant invasion directly to their cubicle, yet they insist the half-eaten sandwich from last month is "still good."

The Credit Taker

HR CLEARED

Collaborative success works best when we recognize each person's contributions!

For the coworker who collects credit like it's a competitive sport. They perfect the art of saying "my project" when describing work they barely glanced at. They strategically step in at the final hour to "help finish up" then present the results to leadership as their brainchild. Their signature move? Interrupting your presentation with "As I was telling the team earlier..." about an idea you shared with them yesterday. They've mastered the confused innocent look when confronted about their credit-snatching ways.

The Perpetual Victim

For the coworker who turns normal workplace events into personal attacks. The printer isn't just out of paper—it ran out specifically to ruin their day. Group deadlines are "unfairly targeting" them. They interpret "Good morning" as hostile depending on tone. Their response to feedback involves dramatic sighs and "Everyone's always against me." Team projects become their personal tragedy theater, complete with whispered asides about how they're being sabotaged by the very concept of teamwork.

The Idea Blocker

HR CLEARED

Building on suggestions with 'yes, and' thinking helps us explore new possibilities!

For the coworker who treats new ideas like personal insults. They've mastered starting sentences with "The problem with that is..." before the proposal is even finished. They've never met a suggestion they couldn't immediately find seventeen flaws in. Their favorite phrases include "We tried something similar in 2005" and "That would never work because..." Their arms remain permanently crossed during brainstorming sessions, their face frozen in a skeptical expression that could curdle milk.

The Meeting Hijacker

YOUR INNER VOICE

Amazing how you turned our website redesign meeting into your TED talk about sourdough starters.

HR CLEARED

Sticking to our agenda helps ensure we address all key topics in our limited time together!

For the coworker who sees meeting agendas as loose suggestions rather than actual plans. They transform a quick project update into their personal stage show. Watch them pivot from quarterly goals to their weekend activities with Olympic-level conversational gymnastics. They're somehow always "just adding something quick" that consumes 30 minutes. The meeting organizer's eye twitch gets more pronounced with each derailment as the scheduled end time whooshes by.

Leverage Resources Jargon

HR CLEARED

Using everyday language makes our communications more accessible and effective for everyone!

For the coworker who can't simply use things—they must "leverage resources" at every turn. They don't make coffee, they "leverage beverage production assets." Simple projects become exercises in "resource optimization leveraging." Their emails read like they swallowed a business textbook and are slowly regurgitating it one buzzword at a time. Watch people's eyes glaze over in meetings as they explain how they plan to "leverage cross-functional synergies" to update the break room fridge schedule.

Paradigm Shift Buzzword

Changing the brand of coffee filters isn't a 'paradigm shift.' It's just coffee.

HR CLEARED

Perhaps we could reserve transformative language for truly significant organizational changes.

For the coworker who sees earth-shattering revolutions in minor workplace tweaks. Updating the font on a memo? "Paradigm shift in communications." Rearranging the supply closet? "Paradigm shift in resource allocation." They drop the phrase into conversations with the frequency of punctuation marks. Everyone silently counts how many times it appears in their presentations, which would make a dangerous drinking game.

Action Item Obsession

For the coworker who treats every conversation like it needs a deliverable. Casual lunch chats end with them assigning deadlines for thoughts you mentioned in passing. They furiously type "ACTION ITEM" in meeting notes when someone says "maybe someday." Their idea of small talk is asking about the status of something you didn't know was your responsibility. Their personal relationships probably involve quarterly performance reviews and improvement metrics.

Best Practices Adherence

YOUR INNER VOICE

These 'best practices' date back to the Stone Age, but sure, let's stick with them.

HR CLEARED

While guidelines are helpful, allowing for innovation often leads to improved processes!

For the coworker who treats "best practices" like sacred texts handed down from corporate Mount Sinai. They shut down suggestions with "that's not best practice" faster than you can finish your sentence. They've printed the company handbook and highlighted it like a religious text. Watch them panic when facing a situation not covered in their best practices bible, freezing like a computer running outdated software. They begin most sentences with "According to best practices..." even when discussing where to order lunch.

The Day Ender

At the end of the day, we still have to listen to you say 'at the end of the day' fifty more times.

Varying our expressions keeps our communications fresh and engaging!

For the coworker who can't complete a thought without this time-based cliché. They start sentences with "At the end of the day..." even at 9 AM. They've used it in meetings, emails, text messages, and probably in their sleep. Team members exchange knowing glances when it inevitably drops, some making tally marks on notepads. The irony? At the actual end of the day, they've communicated very little of substance.

The Win-Win Salesperson

YOUR INNER VOICE

This 'win-win' sounds suspiciously like you winning twice and me getting nothing.

HR CLEARED

Exploring solutions that address various needs can lead to better outcomes!

For the coworker obsessed with finding the mythical "win-win" in every situation. They present obviously one-sided proposals as "win-wins" with a straight face. "You do my work and I take the credit? Win-win!" They've never encountered a conflict they couldn't repackage with this magical phrase. Watch them perform mental gymnastics explaining how staying late to finish their project is somehow a "win" for you.

The Needle Mover

For the coworker who can't simply make progress—they must "move the needle" on everything. Their emails are filled with needle movement aspirations from projects to coffee selection. Watch them in meetings dramatically gesturing with their hands to show exactly how far they've metaphorically pushed this imaginary gauge. They never specify what the needle measures or where it's actually pointing—it's just perpetually moving in their business fantasy world.

The "It Is What It Is" Philosopher

HR CLEARED

Identifying specific improvement opportunities helps us address challenges!

For the coworker who's elevated resignation to an art form. They drop "it is what it is" like a conversation guillotine, instantly killing any hope for solutions. They shrug while saying it, a physical manifestation of giving up. Watch them use it to deflect responsibility, end discussions, and avoid work in one efficient phrase. Their email signature might as well be "Whatever, nothing matters anyway."

The Cat Herder

For the manager who drops "herding cats" into conversation whenever more than two employees need to be in the same meeting. They say it with the weary sigh of someone who believes they're the first person to discover this metaphor. Watch them dramatically collapse into their chair when someone arrives three minutes late, muttering about "these cats" while adjusting their invisible shepherd's crook. The irony? They themselves are often the most unherded cat of all—randomly changing meeting agendas and wandering off-topic.

The Synergy Sorcerer

For the coworker who never collaborates—they only "synergize." They can't simply combine efforts—they must unleash the power of synergy across all platforms and verticals. Their emails read like they're being paid by the buzzword. Watch them in meetings enthusiastically moving their hands together in a merging motion while saying the word. They use it as every part of speech—"Let's synergize!" "That's very synergistic." "I'm feeling particularly synergized today."

The Circle-Back Artist

YOUR INNER VOICE

Your 'circle back' is just code for 'never happening' and we all know it.

HR CLEARED

Setting specific follow-up times helps ensure important topics receive attention!

For the coworker whose favorite conversational escape hatch is promising to "circle back." They've mastered the art of postponing decisions indefinitely through strategic circling. They've created a graveyard of abandoned topics they've promised to revisit. The phrase works like a conversation ejection seat—pushing the parachute button on any topic they'd rather avoid. Their actual circling back success rate hovers around 2%.

The Low-Hanging Fruit Hunter

HR CLEARED

Prioritizing tasks based on specific criteria helps us allocate resources effectively!

For the coworker who sees imaginary orchards of easy wins everywhere. They label projects as "low hanging fruit" despite requiring significant effort. Their favorite meeting contribution is pointing at complex problems and declaring them "practically solved already". Watch them assign these supposedly simple tasks to others while they focus on "strategic thinking." The fruit they identify mysteriously grows higher whenever they're asked to reach for it themselves.

The Box Preacher

Maybe we could think outside the cliché and use original phrases instead.

HR CLEARED

Specific creative approaches often lead to innovative solutions!

For the coworker whose creativity extends only to telling others to be creative. They command everyone to "think outside the box" while firmly remaining inside the most predictable box of business expressions. Watch them draw a box in the air while saying it, complete with hand gestures showing the great beyond of non-box thinking. The irony of using this thoroughly inside-the-box phrase to encourage originality is completely lost on them.

Ooh It's Friday! Ritual

YOUR INNER VOICE

Yes, calendars exist. We're all aware of what day it is.

HR CLEARED

Your enthusiasm for the weekend is contagious! Some of us have varying schedules, though.

For the coworker who acts like they've discovered a new planet every single Friday. They bounce through the office announcing "TGIF!" as if nobody else noticed the date. Their volume increases exponentially as 5 PM approaches. Watch them ask weekend plans with the intensity of a game show host while their colleagues on weekend shifts contemplate hiding under their desks.

Baby-Talking Dog On Mute

HR CLEARED

Double-checking our mute status helps maintain our professional meeting environment!

For the coworker who transformed a budget review into an unexpected pet show. One moment they're silent during a presentation; the next, the entire company hears "WHO'S MY FLOOFY WOOFY BABY? IS SOMEONE A GOOD BOY?" in a voice three octaves higher than their normal speaking tone. Watch them realize their error as twenty squares of horrified faces stare back, followed by the fastest mute button press in recorded history.

Awkward "How Was Your Weekend"

Let's skip this forced small talk where we both lie about how interesting our weekends were.

HR CLEARED

Relaxing and just what I needed—I'm looking forward to applying that renewed energy to our work together.

For the Monday morning ritual that feels like bad community theater. Both parties stick to the script: "Good, yours?" followed by "Fine, thanks" with neither actually listening. The conversation features excessive nodding, awkward pauses, and checking watches. Both people silently pray for a fire alarm or phone call to end this purgatory, knowing they'll repeat the exact same exchange in exactly seven days.

The Coffeemaker Obsessed

HR CLEARED

Your dedication to quality beverages is impressive! Perhaps we could document the process for everyone?

For the coworker who's appointed themselves the unofficial Coffee Czar. They hover near the machine, judging everyone's brewing technique. They've left notes about "proper bean-to-water ratios" and cleaning protocols longer than most legal documents. Watch them physically wince when someone uses the wrong mug or—heaven forbid—leaves less than half an inch in the pot. They refer to the coffeemaker by name and possibly celebrate its birthday.

Bribery With Donuts

For the office tradition of sugar-coated manipulation. The pink box appears mysteriously before requests for overtime, coverage, or fixing someone else's mistakes. Watch the provider strategically mention the donuts in the same breath as "small favor" or "quick request." The transaction is never explicitly stated but perfectly understood: one glazed donut equals one hour of unwanted tasks. The jelly-filled ones are reserved for truly terrible assignments that no one would accept.

The Lunch Hour Assassin

For the coworker who sees your 12–1 PM slot as prime meeting real estate. They've never encountered a lunch break they couldn't transform into a "working lunch" without providing actual food. Watch them say "This will just take 15 minutes" for meetings that inevitably run the full hour. They send invites at 11:55 AM for 12:00 PM meetings, eliminating any chance to decline. They Look confused when you mention eating, as if they've evolved beyond such basic human needs and expected you had too.

The Meeting Room Colonizer

HR CLEARED

Clearing meeting spaces after use helps everyone access shared resources!

For the coworker who treats meeting rooms like newly discovered continents. They leave strategic markers—a jacket draped over a chair, notebooks arranged just so, coffee mug positioned perfectly—to establish ownership of spaces they've booked for 15 minutes but plan to occupy all day. Watch them give hostile glares to anyone who approaches "their" territory despite the room being officially available.

The Dramatic Late Arriver

HR CLEARED

Joining meetings on time helps maintain productive discussion flow!

For the coworker who's never on time but always on stage. They burst into rooms mid-discussion with Oscar-worthy performances of breathlessness and apology. Watch them juggle coffee, laptop, phone and random props while stage-whispering "Sorry! Sorry!" and making eye contact with every single person. Their excuses feature transportation disasters, weather events, or mysterious "back-to-back" meetings nobody else can find on their calendar.

The Format Chaos Agent

HR CLEARED

Consistent formatting helps our audience focus on our important content!

For the coworker whose slides appear to be engaged in a civil war of styles. They mix fonts like they're making a ransom note, with text sizes that change mid-sentence for no reason. Watch them present with zero awareness of the visual nightmare they've created, where each slide introduces new colors, layouts, and possibly violations of physics. They look confused when asked which template they used, answering "All of them?"

The Volunteer Recruiter

HR CLEARED

Clarifying roles and expectations helps team members make informed commitments!

For the coworker who's turned forced volunteering into an art form. They ask "Who wants to handle this?" while suddenly finding their notepad super interesting. They perfect the trick of looking just above everyone's heads while saying "We need someone for this tiny task" that magically grows once you accept. They add "We should probably have a backup person too" before the first victim has even processed their fate. They keep track of who hasn't dodged work lately and target them like a shark smelling blood.

The Progress Illusionist

HR CLEARED

Specific, measurable milestones help demonstrate actual project advancement!

For the coworker who turns status updates into fiction writing. They describe huge breakthroughs that somehow never produce actual results. They excitedly report "major progress" while dodging any real numbers. Their status emails are packed with action verbs that, when decoded, reveal absolutely zero progress. They've perfected making "still at square one" sound like they're changing the world.

The Growth Coach

So my career needs more sunlight and regular watering? Am I an employee or a houseplant?

HR CLEARED

Clear development goals help us track meaningful professional growth!

Perfect for the coworker who can't discuss your career without plant metaphors. They talk about "nurturing your professional roots" instead of giving actual feedback. During reviews, they stare meaningfully at the office fern while explaining how you're "reaching toward the sunlight of opportunity." Ask for specific advancement steps and get a speech about "patience during your career's winter season."

The Potential Prospector

YOUR INNER VOICE

If my 'untapped potential' is so amazing, maybe tap it with an actual promotion?

HR CLEARED

Specific goals help turn potential into measurable achievements!

For the coworker who discusses your "untapped potential" like it's buried treasure they can sense but never dig up. They love vague encouragement: "I see tremendous possibilities for you" followed by zero actual opportunities. During reviews, they look at your current work with slight disappointment before sighing about your untapped potential. You leave meetings feeling simultaneously complimented and criticized, wondering if "potential" means "currently not good enough."

The Timeline Futurist

For the coworker who casually warps the space-time continuum with their deadlines. They describe week-long projects as "quick updates" and use "shouldn't take long" for anything requiring less than 100 hours. Watch them smile serenely while saying, "We need this by Tuesday" about a project that would challenge NASA. When you point out the impossibility, they respond with "I believe in this team," as if team spirit can bend the laws of physics.

The Stakeholder Summoner

For the coworker who treats every email like a popularity contest. They never make decisions when they could instead spawn endless discussion threads. Watch them transform a yes/no question into a company-wide debate by "just copying relevant stakeholders"—which somehow includes people from departments unrelated to the issue. They respond to direct questions with "I'd love to hear what everyone thinks!" followed by adding seven more recipients.

The Problem Ping-Ponger

HR CLEARED

Direct routing helps ensure timely resolution of requests!

For the coworker who plays interdepartmental hot potato with unwanted tasks. They redirect issues with such smooth confidence that no one questions it. Watch them send problems on elaborate journeys: "This should really start with IT, then go to Operations, then Finance for approval, then back to us." They've mastered the art of redirecting so thoroughly that issues eventually return to the original sender, who has forgotten they started the request.

The Responsibility Ghost

YOUR INNER VOICE

Your 'we should consider possibly exploring potential options' contains zero actual commitments.

HR CLEARED

Clear ownership helps ensure accountability for project deliverables!

For the coworker who speaks entirely in non-committal language. They contribute to discussions without ever attaching themselves to actual work. Watch them perfect the art of sounding helpful while promising nothing: "It might be worth thinking about potentially addressing this at some point." Their meeting notes contain countless suggestions but somehow their name never appears in the "owner" column.

The Doorway Blocker

For the coworker who thinks doorways are the perfect spot for spontaneous meetings. They always manage to block the most foot traffic possible while chatting about their weekend plans. Meanwhile, everyone else is left awkwardly side-shuffling to get by, as they obliviously shift just enough to block any other way through. They always seem to pick the worst spots too—like fire exits, bathroom doors, or the tightest part of a hallway.

The Humble Bragger

Oh no, another meeting interrupting your yacht shopping? The struggle is real.

HR CLEARED

Focusing our discussions on work-relevant topics helps maintain productive conversations!

For the coworker who can't mention their beach house without sighing about the "maintenance headaches." Watch them transform a simple "how was your weekend" into a detailed account of their exhausting dinner with celebrities. Their signature move? The pained expression while mentioning how "stressful" their upcoming month in Europe will be.

The IT Crowd Wannabe

HR CLEARED

Our IT team is specially trained to address technical issues safely and effectively!

For the coworker who learned everything they know about computers from crime shows. They swoop in at the first mention of tech trouble, confidently pressing random keys. Watch them dismiss actual solutions with "that never works" before suggesting you "defrag the mainframe." Their advice always includes turning things off and on again, followed by increasingly desperate clicks when that fails.

The Version Control Archaeologist

HR CLEARED

Consistent file naming conventions help
everyone locate the correct documents!

For the coworker who names files like they're writing
diary entries. They create digital fossil records of
folders filled with nearly identical documents. Watch
them share screens and dig through layers of files like
they're on a treasure hunt, muttering "No, not that
one..." over and over. They create a file called "Final_
Final_ACTUALLY_FINAL_USE_THIS_ONE_revised_fixed_
updated_REALLY_FINAL" only to say "Actually, let me
send you the latest version" five minutes later.

The Mundane Storyteller

HR CLEARED

Being mindful of meeting time helps us maintain productive discussions!

For the coworker who narrates their life with excruciating detail. They describe breakfast toast with the intensity of a thriller novel. Watch colleagues frantically invent emergency phone calls as they launch into "So I was at the grocery store yesterday..." followed by a minute-by-minute account of produce selection. Their stories have so many unnecessary details that listeners age visibly waiting for the nonexistent punchline.

The Enthusiastic Hand-Talker

HR CLEARED

Being mindful of our physical space helps create a safe environment for everyone!

For the coworker whose hands operate independently from their spatial awareness. Their enthusiasm cannot be contained to mere words—it requires a three-foot gesture radius. Watch them accidentally swat phones, knock over drinks, and nearly slap passing colleagues while describing their weekend. Their most dangerous move? The "dramatic point" that transforms into accidental jabbing of nearby innocents.

The Compliment Fisher

HR CLEARED

Direct questions help us provide the specific feedback you're looking for!

For the coworker who's turned fishing for compliments into an art form. They present their work with "I don't know if this is any good," while scanning the room for praise. Their signature technique? Dropping a self-deprecating comment that lingers awkwardly until someone feels forced to respond with a compliment. They've perfected the act of looking bummed about totally normal things until the validation rolls in.

The Printer Whisperer

For the coworker who believes technology responds to emotional appeals. They treat printer troubleshooting as a hostage negotiation, pleading with the machine while ignoring obvious error messages. Watch them stroke the paper tray while whispering "come on, buddy" as if gentle encouragement will materialize toner. Their desperate monologues include personal appeals, threats, and eventually existential questions about why the universe is against them.

The Cubicle Conversationalist

For the coworker who believes cubicle walls are soundproof. They yell conversations across the office instead of using phones, chat, or their legs. Watch them shout "HEY LINDA, DID YOU SEE THAT EMAIL ABOUT THE BUDGET CUTS?" while everyone pretends not to hear the confidential information. Their volume settings range from "unnecessarily loud" to "potential hearing damage," with special talent for increasing volume when topics become more sensitive.

The Desk Mirror Gazelle

For the coworker who treats their desk as a beauty salon. They've established a dedicated mirror workspace for continuous appearance monitoring. Watch them contort into elaborate poses to check different angles while pretending to work. Their workday includes scheduled reflection check-ins that increase in frequency before meetings. They maintain unbroken eye contact with themselves while accidentally ignoring actual humans trying to speak with them.

The Pun-ishment Provider

HR CLEARED

Reading the room helps ensure our humor resonates with everyone!

For the coworker whose humor peaked at dad jokes. They transform every innocent conversation into an opportunity for wordplay warfare. Watch them derail important discussions to announce they're "Excel-ing at spreadsheets today." Their eyes light up with mischievous glee seconds before unleashing puns that trigger physical pain. They interpret groans as encouragement and keep a mental scorecard of how many people they made cringe before lunch.

The Blame Shifter

HR CLEARED

Focusing on solutions helps us address challenges constructively!

For the coworker with supernatural reflexes for avoiding accountability. They deploy blame faster than their own shadow. Watch them transform "I forgot to send the email" into an elaborate conspiracy involving IT failures, time zones, and possibly solar flares. Their linguistic gymnastics ensure they're never the subject of any sentence describing errors. They've perfected looking genuinely victimized by circumstances they completely controlled.

The Excuse Generator

For the coworker whose excuses deserve their own creative writing award. They transform simple missed deadlines into epic tales of tragedy and triumph. Watch them explain late work with increasingly elaborate scenarios involving traffic accidents, power outages, and surprise visits from distant relatives. Their excuses feature more plot twists than thriller novels, all delivered with unflinching sincerity and increasingly implausible details.

The Bathroom Conversationalist

HR CLEARED

Respecting personal boundaries helps maintain comfortable workplace interactions!

For the coworker who believes bathroom etiquette includes detailed conversation. They initiate discussions through stall walls about weekend plans and quarterly reports. Watch them maintain uninterrupted eye contact in the mirror while discussing project timelines during handwashing. Their signature move? The awkward over-the-urinal-divider question about lunch plans that forces you to speed-pee to escape the conversational ambush.

The Late-Night Emailer

For the coworker whose productivity peaks when everyone else is asleep. They send non-urgent emails exclusively during vampire hours. Watch them follow up at 8:01 AM asking "Did you see my email?" about the message sent four hours earlier. They mark routine updates as "URGENT" at midnight, then expressing genuine confusion about why you didn't respond immediately to their thoughts on the office snack selection.

Ready For More Fun?
(Of course you do)

Enjoyed this guide to corporate survival? Your journey to laughing out loud isn't over yet.

Check out these books:

HR Stamped Ways to Say Things I Can't Say Out Loud at Work
This HR-blessed translation guide turns your inner screams into promotion-worthy poetry.

And when you need a break from office politics...

150 Puzzles While You Poop
Proven Ways to Unleash Bursts of Genius on Your Throne

<u>More humor books and fun activity books coming soon!</u>
<u>(We know you need them to stay sane)</u>

Find all our books at major online bookstores! (Just type these exact titles into search bar)

www.ingramcontent.com/pod-product-compliance
Lightning Source LLC
Chambersburg PA
CBHW071213120626
46546CB00006B/2536